Office of the Special Project Facilitator's

Lessons Learned

Sri Lanka Integrated Road Investment Program

ADB

© 2020 Asian Development Bank
6 ADB Avenue, Mandaluyong City, 1550 Metro Manila, Philippines
Tel +63 2 8632 4444; Fax +63 2 8636 2444
www.adb.org

Some rights reserved. Published in 2020.

ISBN 978-92-9262-405-7 (print); 978-92-9262-406-4 (electronic); 978-92-9262-407-1 (ebook)
Publication Stock No. ARM200271-2
DOI: http://dx.doi.org/10.22617/ARM200271-2

Note:
In this publication, "$" refers to United States dollars and "SLR" refers to Sri Lankan rupees.

On the cover: Batayaya–Kandilpana–Bevaraliya road in Matara District, rehabilitated and improved under iRoad program (photo by RDA).

Contents

Tables, Figures, and Map

Tables

Figures

Map

Acknowledgments

The Office of the Special Project Facilitator's (OSPF) *Lessons Learned* series featuring Sri Lanka's Integrated Road Investment Program is a collaborative effort led by Sushma Kotagiri, principal facilitation specialist, OSPF and Aruna Uddeeptha Nanayakkara, senior project officer (transport), Sri Lanka Resident Mission (SLRM). Chamindra Weerackody, OSPF consultant, contributed to the research and preliminary writing. The case study greatly benefited from the contributions, comments, discussions, and support of various professionals—Ranjith Pemasiri, secretary, Ministry of Roads and Highways; Jennifer Weerakoon, project director, iRoad Program; Anil Perera, team leader, iRoad construction supervision consultants; Manjula Amerasinghe, principal environment specialist, East Asia Department (former officer-in-charge, SLRM); Saranga Gajasinghe, safeguard officer, SLRM; Mary Jane David, senior consultation officer, OSPF (content and structure); Wilfredo Agliam, associate facilitation coordinator, OSPF (administration and coordination with all the participating agencies and stakeholders); Joy Gatmaytan (editor); and Michelle Ortiz (design and layout).

The team greatly appreciates the advice and guidance received from Warren Evans, special project facilitator, OSPF; Sri Widowati, former country director; and Chen Chen, country director, SLRM during the analytical work and publication process.

Abbreviations

ADB	–	Asian Development Bank
AP	–	affected people
CRP	–	Compliance Review Panel
CSD	–	context-sensitive design
DS	–	Divisional Secretary
DSD	–	Divisional Secretary's Division
ESDD	–	Environmental and Social Development Division
GN	–	Grama Niladhari
GND	–	Grama Niladhari Division
GRC	–	Grievance Redress Committee
GRM	–	grievance redress mechanism
iRoad	–	Integrated Road Investment Program
km	–	kilometer
OSPF	–	Office of the Special Project Facilitator
PIC	–	project implementation consultant
PIU	–	project implementation unit
RDA	–	Road Development Authority
SLRM	–	Sri Lanka Resident Mission
SLR	–	Sri Lanka rupee
STDP	–	Southern Transport Development Project
TA	–	technical assistance

I. Introduction

The Asian Development Bank (ADB) envisions a prosperous, inclusive, resilient, and sustainable Asia and the Pacific, while sustaining its efforts to eradicate extreme poverty in the region. It assists its members and partners by providing loans, technical assistance (TA), grants, and equity investments to promote social and economic development.

ADB maximizes the development impact of its assistance by facilitating policy dialogues; providing advisory services; and mobilizing financial resources through cofinancing operations that tap official, commercial, and export credit sources.

Workers maintaining road under ADB-funded Integrated Road Investment Program (photo by RDA).

*The problem-solving function is outcome driven. It focuses on **finding ways to address the problems of the affected people.***

Accountability Mechanism

To ensure the proper and timely implementation of its projects, ADB has set up the Accountability Mechanism, a forum where people adversely affected by ADB-assisted projects can seek solutions to their problems and report alleged noncompliance with ADB's operational policies and procedures. It consists of two separate but complementary functions: problem-solving and compliance review.

The Office of the Special Project Facilitator (OSPF) is responsible for the problem-solving function of ADB's Accountability Mechanism. It aims to actively respond to the concerns of people affected by ADB-assisted projects through fair, transparent, and consensus-based problem solving. The problem-solving function is outcome driven. It focuses on finding ways to address the problems of the affected people (AP). OSPF works closely and collaboratively with the concerned operations departments and government counterparts for eligible complaints to find satisfactory solutions that are mutually acceptable to all concerned parties.

The compliance review function is done by the Compliance Review Panel (CRP). It is a fact-finding body of the ADB Board of Directors. People who are directly, materially, and adversely affected by an ADB-assisted project during formulation, processing, or implementation can file a request for compliance review with the independent CRP which investigates compliance with ADB's operational policies and procedures.

Project-affected people can choose whether they want to go to the problem-solving or the compliance review function.

Complaints are filed with the complaint receiving officer who informs and gives copy of the complaints to the OSPF and CRP heads. The complainants are given 21 days within which to decide which function they prefer to handle their complaints. The complaint is then forwarded to the preferred party.

Safeguard Policy Statement

The Safeguard Policy Statement (SPS) 2009 describes common objectives of ADB's safeguards, lays out policy principles, and outlines the delivery process for ADB's safeguard policy. It builds upon the safeguard policies on the environment, involuntary resettlement, and indigenous peoples, and brings them into one single policy that enhances consistency and coherence, and more comprehensively addresses environmental and social impacts and risks.

The SPS aims to promote sustainability of project outcomes by (i) protecting the environment and people from the adverse impacts of projects on the environment and APs, where possible; (ii) minimizing, mitigating, and/or compensating for adverse project impacts on the environment and APs when avoidance is not possible; and (iii) helping borrowers/clients to strengthen their safeguard systems and develop their capacity to manage environmental and social risks.

Grievance Redress Mechanism

Complaints and grievances go through a grievance redress mechanism (GRM) that is a combination of institutions, instruments, methods, and processes by which resolution of a grievance is sought and provided.[1] It is intended to provide a predictable, transparent, and credible process to all parties, resulting in outcomes that are fair, effective, and lasting.[2] This facilitates resolution of AP's concerns and grievances about the borrower's/client's social and environmental performance at the project level. The GRM should be scaled to the risks and impacts of the project and should address AP's concerns and complaints promptly, using an understandable and transparent process that is gender responsive, culturally appropriate, and readily accessible to all segments of the AP.[3]

Methodology of the Study

OSPF conducted analytical work of selected GRMs and problem-solving processes established by ADB-assisted projects in their respective countries.

The objectives of the case study is to:

(i) review the institutional arrangements and processes established by ADB-assisted projects for handling grievances and complaints reported by APs during project planning and implementation;

(ii) assess the efficiency and effectiveness of the GRMs in grievance handling and identify the lessons learned and good practices in grievance redress that can be replicated in similar contexts;

(iii) produce a knowledge product based on empirical evidence elicited from the case study that will provide valuable insights and guidance to project-based grievance redress processes; and

(iv) use the case study for GRM training programs designed for ADB staff and project implementing agencies.

*The GRM should be scaled to the risks and impacts of the project and should address AP's concerns and complaints promptly, using an **understandable and transparent process that is gender responsive, culturally appropriate, and readily accessible to all segments of the AP.***

---

[1] Center for European Policy Analysis. 2009. *A Review of the Southern Transport Development Project.* Colombo.

[2] International Finance Corporation. 2008. *Advisory Note: A Guide to Designing and Implementing Grievance Mechanisms for Development Projects.* Washington, D.C.

[3] ADB. 2009. *Safeguard Policy Statement.* Manila.

In consultation with the Sri Lanka Resident Mission, OSPF selected two projects for the studies, one of which is the Integrated Road Investment Program (iRoad) implemented by the Road Development Authority (RDA).

The case study approach was largely qualitative. Document reviews, secondary data collection, and individual interviews conducted with selected project staff and consultants, and the complainants constituted the key components of the methodology adopted for the case study. It is based on information and data collected from two project implementing areas: the Southern Province and the Kegalle District in the Sabaragamuwa Province. Southern Province comprises three districts—Galle, Matara, and Hambantota. The Sabaragamuwa Province includes Kegalle and Ratnapura districts. Secondary data on the implementation of GRM and problem-solving processes were taken from project-related documents such

as the resettlement framework, facility administration manual of the iRoad program, semiannual social safeguards monitoring reports, and databases and master registries maintained to record the complaints and grievances in the Southern Province and Kegalle District. However, field visits to sites where the grievances and complaints were raised and interviews with the complainants were confined to Matara District in the South and Kegalle District in Sabaragamuwa. Interviews conducted with resident engineers; project engineers; construction engineers; social, gender, and resettlement specialists; environmental specialists; environmental and social safeguards officers; contractor's management staff; and the team leader of the project implementation consultant (PIC) in the Southern Province were all helpful in capturing their personal experiences with other districts as well.

II. The Project: Integrated Road Investment Program

Description

iRoad commenced in 2014 to rehabilitate and develop several selected rural, provincial, and national roads, and increase their transport efficiency (map). The program will serve as a tool for poverty alleviation, improving the connectivity between rural communities and the socioeconomic centers, and allowing poor people in the area to directly access other areas of the country to engage in social and economic activities. It will facilitate linkages between production centers and marketplaces; increase mobility of people; facilitate access to social, health, and education infrastructure; and generate new employment opportunities.[4] It has two phases: iRoad 1 was approved by ADB in September 2014 and is scheduled to be completed in September 2024, and iRoad 2 which was launched in September 2017 will continue until September 2027.

A road improved under iRoad program in Nuwara Eliya, Central province Sri Lanka (photo by RDA).

---

[4] Government of Sri Lanka, Ministry of Highways and Roads Development. 2019. Social Monitoring Report: Road Investment Program in Sri Lanka PIC (03) Central and Sabaragamuwa Provinces and Kalutara District in Western Province (prepared by ADB).

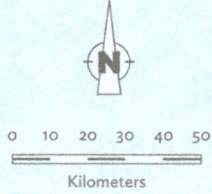

SRI LANKA
INTEGRATED ROAD INVESTMENT PROGRAM
(iRoad 1 and 2 Programs)

—— iRoad 1 Project
—— iRoad 2 Project
==== Expressway
—— Class A National Road
✪ National Capital
◉ Chief Provincial Town
—·—·— District Boundary
Boundaries are not necessarily authoritative.

Palk Strait

Jaffna

Palk Bay

Gulf of Mannar

Trincomalee

Bay of Bengal

Anuradhapura

Kurunegala

Kandy

Badulla

Colombo
SRI JAYAWARDENEPURA KOTTE

Ratnapura

Galle

INDIAN OCEAN

N

0 10 20 30 40 50
Kilometers

Under iRoad 1, several rural roads in Sabaragamuwa; Southern, Central, North Central, and North Western provinces; and Kalutara District in the Western Province will be developed and maintained. iRoad 2 covers Uva and Northern, Eastern, and Western provinces of the country. The Ministry of Roads and Highways (since November 2019)[5] is the executing agency of the program while its implementing agency is the RDA. The Environmental and Social Development Division (ESDD) of RDA is involved in the program and assists the safeguards teams of the project implementation units (PIU) in the project implementing provinces. It also supports its consultants in conducting sample socioeconomic surveys, impact assessments, safeguards planning, and joint monitoring. The ESDD was set up by RDA to strengthen environmental and social safeguards management in road projects, after the experience and lessons learned from the Southern Transport Development Project (STDP). The program started its implementation in 2015.

iRoad is implemented in several Grama Niladhari Divisions (GNDs)[6] of the abovementioned five provinces and in one district of the Western Province. The areas were selected based on their population, development potential, and distance to trunk road network. Enhancement of the connectivity is to be achieved by (i) improving rural access roads linking the rural hubs to trunk road network so that the roads will be able to withstand all-weather conditions, and (ii) operating a sustainable trunk road network, encompassing national roads, that will be able to withstand at least fair condition. Development of the roads to withstand all-weather conditions will improve rural access, and link rural hubs to the national road network. It will improve and strengthen the national highways network efficiency thereby achieving smooth traffic flow, reduced travel time and costs, and increased lifetime of the roads through appropriate and periodic maintenance.[7]

iRoad does not foresee any involuntary land acquisitions for rural road improvements, and hence neither economic nor physical displacements. Road improvements are mainly carried out within the existing right of way which is from 3 meters (m) to 5.5 m. However, in some instances, it is required to take marginal strips of land from adjacent ones mainly to improve road safety and drainage aspects to comply with the road design. Voluntary land donation is the concept that has been adopted in the iRoad program for taking small land strips.[8]

The contractor is responsible for the completion of the road rehabilitation and improvement works within a period of 2 years, and performance-based maintenance for another 3 years. Rehabilitation works include improving pavements or road surface; constructing side drains and embankments; and improving culverts, causeways, and bridges.[9]

One of the key features of iRoad is it endeavors to build a sense of ownership among the rural communities for road

One of the key features of iRoad is it endeavors to build a sense of ownership among the rural communities for road improvement projects in their area and to encourage their participation in road designing and planning, road rehabilitation works, and their maintenance.

[5] Formerly Ministry of Higher Education and Highways (later Highways and Road Development and Petroleum Resources Development) until November 2019.

[6] The smallest administrative unit at the village level in Sri Lanka.

[7] ADB. 2014. *Sri Lanka: Integrated Road Investment Program: Resettlement Framework.* Manila.

[8] Road Development Authority. 2018. ADB-funded Integrated Road Investment Program. A Program to Improve Connectivity of Rural Communities and Socioeconomic Centers.

[9] ADB. 2014. *Sri Lanka: Integrated Road Investment Program: Resettlement Framework.* Manila.

The GRCs provide a comfortable environment for the complainants as they are assisted by local administrators with whom they regularly interact for their administrative needs.

improvement projects in their area and to encourage their participation in road designing and planning, road rehabilitation works, and their maintenance.

The program realized the strategic importance of tapping the social capital that exists in the communities for efficient project implementation. Unlike in the typical road development projects in which the approach is largely top-down and dominated by engineering and technical cadres, iRoad ensured strong community engagement throughout the project cycle. This move to deviate from the conventional approach was based on the experience in handling a previous project also in Sri Lanka. Recognition on the part of project planners and implementers to push for community engagement could be credited to the experience gained from the STDP which was also implemented by RDA and jointly funded by ADB and the Japan Bank for International Cooperation/Japan International Cooperation Agency. The project completion report of STDP noted that "the STDP is an invaluable source of lessons for mega road project planning and implementation".[10]

Project Grievance Redress Mechanism

Institutional Framework

The resettlement framework of iRoad provided for the establishment of a two-tier GRM to address grievances and complaints reported by APs during project implementation. The proposed structure of the GRM is uniform across all iRoad projects and requires its establishment for each one. The first level of the GRM is the Grievance Redress Committee (GRC) set up at the GND level, while its second level is the GRC formed at the Divisional Secretary's Division (DSD level).[11] Grievances and complaints that are complex in nature and cannot be resolved at the GND-level GRC are forwarded to the DSD-level GRC for resolution. The GRCs provide a comfortable environment for the complainants as they are assisted by local administrators with whom they regularly interact for their administrative needs. Table 1 shows the composition of the GRCs at both GND and DSD level.

Table 1: Composition of the Grievance Redress Committee	
GND Level GRC	**DSD Level GRC**
Grama Niladhari[12] of the area (chairperson)	Divisional Secretary of the area (chairperson)
Representative of the PIU (secretary)	Representative of the PIU (secretary)
Representative of the supervision consultant	Grama Niladhari of the area where the grievance/complaint originated
Representative of the contractor	Representative of the supervision consultant
A community member or religious leader	Representative of the contractor
A female representative from the local community	A representative of a social organization of the area
	A community member or religious leader
	A female representative from the local community

DSD = Divisional Secretary's Division, GND = Grama Niladhari Division, GRC = Grievance Redress Committee, PIU = project implementation unit.

Source: Road Development Authority.

---

[10] ADB. 2014. *Completion Report: Southern Transport Development Project in Sri Lanka.* Manila.
[11] The DSD is an administrative sub-unit of a district comprising several GNDs and serving the needs of people in those GNDs.
[12] Administrative head of the GND.

Apart from being members of the GRCs, the Grama Niladhari (GN) or the Divisional Secretary (DS) also invites local level development officers or officers from concerned government departments to GRC meetings depending on the nature of the complaint and the type of issues to be addressed. For example, at GND-level GRCs, the GN invites and consults the other village level government officers such as the agrarian research and production assistant, economic development officer, etc. to get their views and suggestions on the issues to be resolved. At DSD-level GRC, the DS also invites and consults the divisional-level officers such as the medical officer of health, environmental officer of the Central Environmental Authority, disaster management officer, irrigation engineer, and whoever is deemed important to the problem-solving process. At the GRC, the contractor is represented by the environmental safeguards officer. The secretary of both GRCs is the project engineer of the PIU who coordinates the meetings, invites the members to the meetings, and documents the proceedings and decisions of the GRCs at each level. Decisions of the GRCs are communicated to the complainants by the project engineer who is provided with additional coordination support by social and environmental officers and the assistants of the PIU. The composition of the GRCs is gender responsive with a growing number of female GNs and DSs serving in their respective divisions. The gender representation is further strengthened by female representatives from local communities. Participation of GRC members is voluntary and none of the members are paid any allowances for their sittings in the GRCs.

As mentioned earlier, the resettlement framework of the project prescribed only a two-tier GRM. However, the facility administration manual of the project (July 2014) provides for a three-tier GRM depending on the nature and significance of the complaints and grievances to be addressed. The three levels constitute the project's site level, the GND level, and the DSD level:

(i) at grassroot/site level, complaints will be directly received and addressed by the contractor, the PIC, or PIU representative on-site;

(ii) grievances that are simple but cannot be addressed at the grassroot/site level will be addressed at the GND level; and

(iii) more complex grievances that cannot be addressed at the GND level will be addressed at the DSD level.[13]

Complaints and grievances that cannot be resolved at these three levels are addressed at the provincial level with the intervention of the provincial chief secretary. So far, there have been few complaints that were elevated to the provincial level.

The iRoad in the South has social and environmental safeguards officers who perform a significant role in the grievance redress and problem-solving processes, especially in conducting consultations with complainants, participating at GRC meetings, documenting GRC outcomes, and assisting PIU and the contractor to reach amicable settlements with the complainants. At the PIU level, the safeguards officers comprise an environment safeguards officer, an environment safeguards assistant, a social safeguards officer, and a social safeguards assistant. The composition of the safeguards staff of the PIC includes a social, gender,

13 ADB. 2014. Sri Lanka: Integrated Road Investment Program. Updated Facility Administration Manual. (updated in March 2018).

and resettlement specialist; a social, gender, and resettlement assistant; an environment specialist; and an environment officer. Apart from the above, each district-level resident engineer is assigned an environmental assistant. Further, each contractor employs an environment safeguards officer and one safety officer. The social safeguards and environment assistants are young university graduates with a majority from rural areas. The program provided them with several rounds of capacity-building training on safeguards management. The program's investment in this capacity building, especially in the management of social and environmental safeguards, significantly contribute to timely and efficient handling of grievances that spreads over a wider geographical area and cuts across many communities with diverse socioeconomic and political dynamics.

Channels of Grievance Communication

Linked to the community engagement and context-sensitive design (CSD), another important feature of iRoad is its efforts of preventing or minimizing complaints and grievances. This is achieved through sharing of information with the community; listening to people's concerns, requests, and suggestions; accommodating them in project designs and implementation; and creating a sense of community ownership to the project. People began to perceive the rehabilitated roads as *ape paara* (our road) and not as *anduwe paara* (government road) as an expression of their feeling of inclusiveness. They are able to resolve their issues collectively and amicably without reporting to external parties. Thus, while establishing a GRM to resolve reported complaints and grievances, iRoad also adopted an innovative approach which significantly

Road design and construction through concept of CSD—design and build roads considering public requests and suggestions (photo by RDA).

contributed to grievance prevention. iRoad has been conducting awareness-raising events for project implementing agency staff, project consultants, and contractor on the importance of grievance prevention and handling. At these events, Sri Lanka Resident Mission shares copies of the ADB publication titled Designing and Implementing Grievance Redress Mechanisms—A *Guide for Implementers of Transport Projects in Sri Lanka*. A TA consultant was also engaged to reach out to the complainants either personally or via telephone within 24 hours upon receipt of a complaint for an initial consultation to explore remedial measures.

Information on the establishment and operational modalities of the GRM is first communicated to the local communities at the inception of individual road projects where community awareness-raising programs are conducted. These programs focus on sharing information on the nature of the project, the extent to which the community can participate, and the procedures for reporting grievances and complaints. Such programs are complemented by notices printed in local languages and displayed at strategic locations where the public are gathered, such as the office of the GN[14] and other places along the

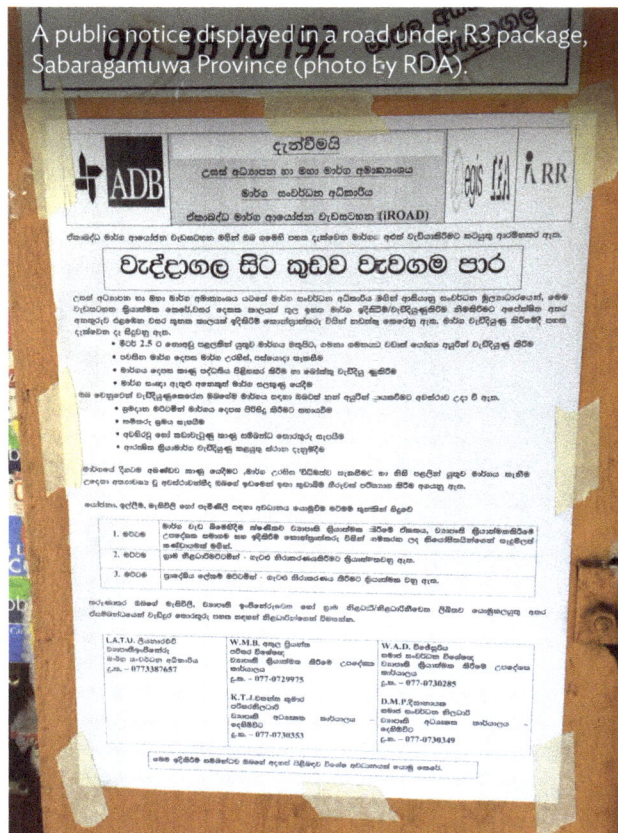

A public notice displayed in a road under R3 package, Sabaragamuwa Province (photo by RDA).

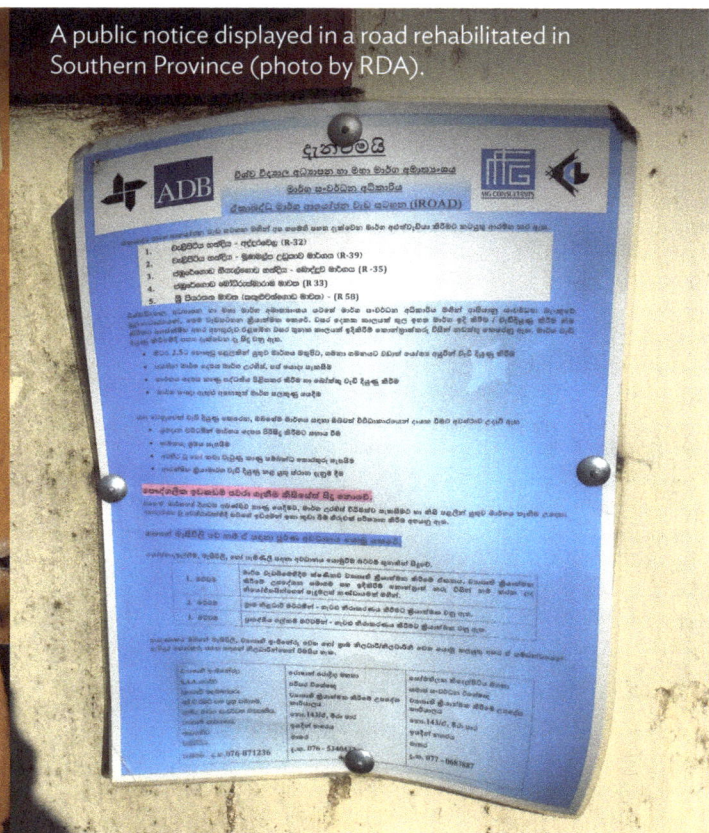

A public notice displayed in a road rehabilitated in Southern Province (photo by RDA).

[14] The administrative officer appointed by the government to the village level.

roads where such notices will easily attract attention. The notices also provide the names of contact persons (e.g., social, gender, and resettlement specialist; environment specialist; project engineer; etc.) and their telephone numbers in case the APs have grievances to report. The environmental and social safeguards officers of PIC continue to monitor that these notices remain posted throughout project implementation period.

APs use multiple channels to report their grievances, complaints, requests, and suggestions. The personnel who directly receive complaints and grievances include the staff members of PIU, PIC, and contractor; the DS; the GN; and sometimes, the political authority. Complainants may also drop their complaints in the complaint and suggestion boxes placed at key locations of the road under rehabilitation and in the offices of the contractor and the GN.

In the South, complaints placed inside the complaint and suggestion boxes are collected once a week by the resident engineer's environment assistant, whereas in Kegalle, these are collected by the environment safeguards officer of the contractor. However, the practice of placing complaints in the complaint and suggestion box gradually diminished as the communities have built rapport with the field staff of either PIU or the contractor. APs submit their written or verbal complaints directly to the field staff or their respective offices. They also make verbal complaints to the staff of the contractor. Complainants who report their grievances verbally (e.g., telephone, short messaging service [SMS], etc.) are required to submit a written complaint later once the project team has established the eligibility of the complaints.

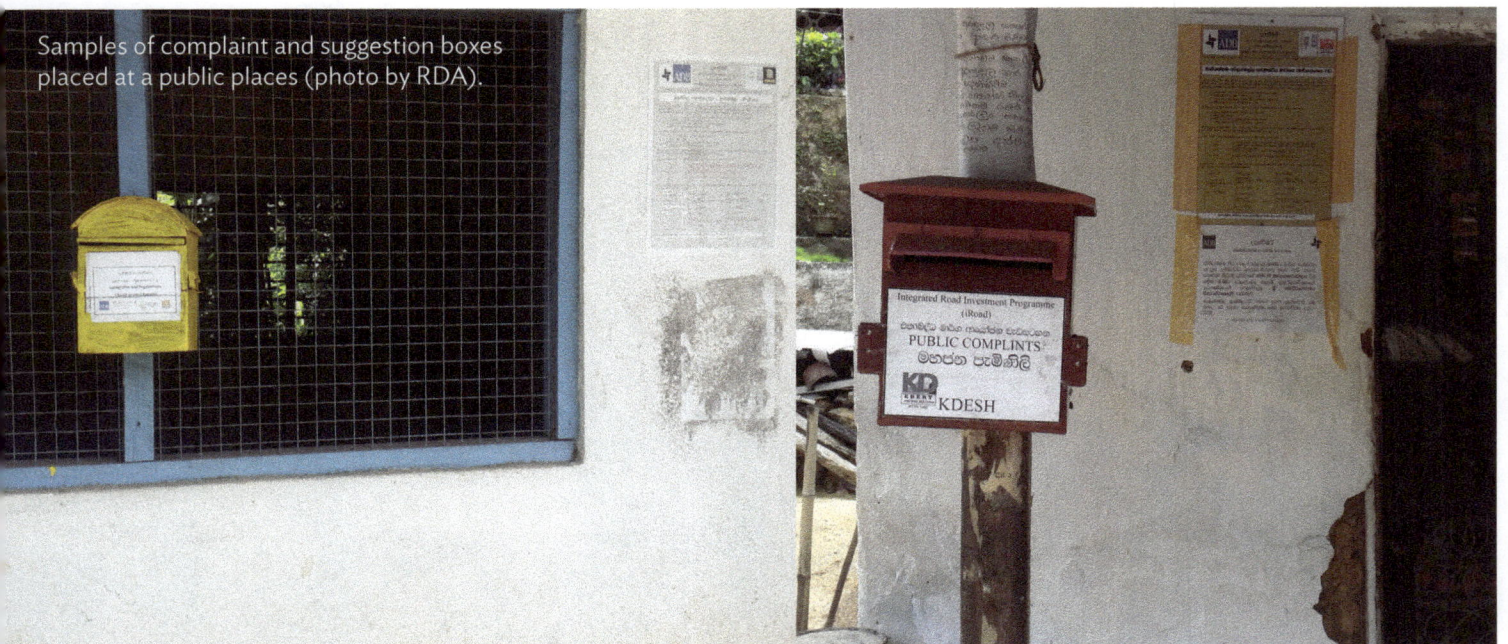

Samples of complaint and suggestion boxes placed at a public places (photo by RDA).

In addition to the abovementioned channels of communication, complainants can also submit their grievances through the official website (www.iroadinfo.rda.gov.lk/publiccontact) of the project coordinating and implementing unit based in Colombo.

There have been few instances when complaints were directly reported to the Sri Lanka Resident Mission and ADB headquarters. One example was when the road widening caused unsafe environment for a household who has a disabled child. The household complained to the resident mission and ADB and asked for a retaining wall. The PIC inspected the site and proposed a design for a retaining wall to secure the complainant's house from possible earth slips, and the contractor built the wall accordingly. After 6 months, the complainant wrote to the resident mission again and asked for a retaining wall covering her entire land. In this instance, ADB's TA consultant , together with a team from PIU, PIC, and the contractor, visited this location a few times and explained to the complainant that protection to the house had been adequately provided and that arrangements should just be made to divert the storm water away from the embankment.

Complainants who are dissatisfied with the grievance redress and problem-solving processes either at the site level or through the formal GRM can seek redress through *samatha mandala* (mediation boards) established under the Ministry of Justice, Human Rights Commission, or the judiciary. APs can also report their grievances to ADB's Accountability Mechanism.

Grievance Registration

Public grievances, complaints, requests, and suggestions received by various agencies mentioned above either verbally or in writing will be finally directed to the project manager of the contractor. The environment safeguards officer of the contractor will register these complaints, grievances, requests, and suggestions and enter the information in the master registry as well as the electronic database.

All information is maintained according to the contract package and individual roads. Moreover, a printed format is used to register the complaints and grievances. Thereafter, these registered complaints and grievances are forwarded to the project engineer by the environment officer. The following information is included in the GRM database:

(i)   reference number of the complaint;

(ii)   road identification number;

(iii) name of the road;

(iv) date of the complaint;

(v)   name of the agency or person who initially received the complaint or whether it was placed in a complaint box;

(vi) mode of reporting the complaint, whether written or verbal;

(vii) details of the complainant (name, address, contact telephone number);

(viii) brief description of the complaint and location (chainage);

(ix) status of the action taken to resolve the issue
  a. whether a solution has been agreed on;
  b. whether the solutions are being implemented; and
  c. whether the issue has been resolved; and
(x) complainant's satisfaction over the resolution and other remarks and observations.

The printed form used in Kegalle has provisions to record the feedback from the complainant at the end of the problem-solving process, and whether the complainant is satisfied with the resolution. In the same manner, the form also records reasons for any dissatisfaction.

A format used in recording grievances/complaints (photo by RDA).

Grievance Classification

Both in the Southern Province and Kegalle District, issues reported by APs or project beneficiaries are segregated into three to four categories. In Kegalle, the categories are (i) complaints, (ii) requests, and (iii) suggestions. In the South, they are (i) grievances, (ii) complaints, (iii) requests, and (iv) suggestions. These categories are defined in Table 2.

The suggestions and requests submitted to the GRM by the villagers emanate from the first interaction that the program staff have with the villagers immediately after the commencement of the civil works by the contractor. This initial interaction, as described earlier, is the CSD process where the contractor's design engineers, the project implementing agency's project engineers, and the staff of PIC meet the villagers to consult them on their opinions and suggestions on road improvement. Additionally, villagers are also consulted on ways to minimize adverse environment, social, and construction-related impacts that may result from roads

rehabilitation works. The CSD stage also provides an opportunity for the technical and engineering design teams to tap into the local indigenous knowledge and incorporate them into their technical designs. This consultation process encourages the villagers to continuously send their suggestions and requests for road improvements.

The program staff and consultants believe that requests and suggestions received from people cannot be disregarded completely as these have the potential to escalate into either complaints or grievances at a later stage. Therefore, the GRM maintains the records of these requests and suggestions, though sometimes, not all of them can be addressed within the scope of the project. In some instances, these requests and suggestions are forwarded to the relevant local government authorities for implementation. In the Southern Province, the project invested more than SLR389.70 million to accommodate the requests and suggestions from the community to change the road designs. It was reported that 120 design changes were

*The CSD stage also provides an opportunity for the technical and engineering design teams **to tap into the local indigenous knowledge and incorporate them into their technical designs.***

Table 2: Definitions of Grievances, Complaints, Requests, and Suggestions

Category	Definitions
Grievances	A written or verbal communication by the public to PIA (i.e., RDA), PIC, or contractor about the hardships that a person, family, or group of people has to undergo due to project activities.
Complaints	A written or verbal communication by a stakeholder or a beneficiary to PIA (i.e., RDA), PIC or contractor on the dissatisfaction over a direct or indirect impact of an activity conducted during road development.
Requests	A reasonable written or verbal communication by a stakeholder or a beneficiary to the PIA (i.e., RDA), PIC, or contractor to consider providing additional materials or services within the scope of the project.
Suggestions	A written or verbal communication of a new plan or idea outside the project's scope by a stakeholder or beneficiary to PIA (i.e., RDA), PIC, or contractor.

PIA = project implementing agency, PIC = project implementation consultant, RDA = Road Development Authority.
Source: RDA.

effected to 60 roads in the province.[15] In the Kegalle District, the total amount spent on addressing public requests was more than SLR16.20 million.[16] These comprise requests for house access, additional retaining walls, culverts, concrete drains, dish drains, etc.

In addition, issues related to cracks caused to structures due to vibration or use of heavy machinery are maintained separately. This is largely for the convenience of monitoring the restoration work of the damaged structures which also requires the intervention and payment of compensation by the contractor's insurance agent. Restoration of damages caused to structures takes a relatively longer period, and in some instances, compensation covered by the insurance is hardly sufficient for the complete restoration. In such situations, the contractor will provide either additional cash compensation or material assistance to bridge the gap. Or, PIU uses its provisional funds under 'demolishing and re-building properties' to compensate for cracks.

Problem-Solving Process

The site level is the lowest level of the GRM. It is also the first focal point that receives complaints, grievances, requests, and suggestions from the AP or the general public.

The project engineer performs a key role in the grievance redress process both at the site level and GRM level. When a complaint is received, the project engineer together with the construction engineer; social and environmental officers of the PIU, and the environment assistant of the resident engineer; and the environment safeguards officer of the contractor immediately meet with the complainant for a consultation. During this initial consultation, the project team tries to gain a better understanding of the problem and its root causes. Some consultations may extend to several rounds. With a clear understanding of the problem, the team proposes a solution for the grievance provided the solution is within the scope of the project and funds are available to implement it.

The resident engineer or the assistant resident engineer and their respective environment assistants, also assist the project engineer and the team to reach an amicable settlement. In some instances, the project engineer also consults the team leader and the social and environmental specialists of the PIC and seek their assistance in the problem-solving process. The project engineer also coordinates with the contractor and his or her staff in implementing remedial measures.

If an immediate solution cannot be offered, the project engineer will explain the situation to the complainant. When an agreement is reached, an exact time frame is agreed on for implementation. However, in some instances, such time frames cannot be stipulated particularly when proposed solutions require modifications to technical designs or allocation of additional resources. In such

---

15 Government of Sri Lanka, Ministry of Highways and Road Department. 2019. Social Monitoring Report: Integrated Road Investment Program in Sri Lanka PIC 01 - Southern Province (prepared by ADB).

16 Government of Sri Lanka, Ministry of Highways and Road Department. 2019. Social Monitoring Report: Integrated Road Investment Program in Sri Lanka Tranches 2, 3, and 4 PIC 03 - Sabaragamuwa and Central Provinces and Kalutara district (prepared by ADB).

Spraying of water to control dust (photo by RDA).

A joint site visit conducted with Divisional Secretary and iRoad team (photo by RDA).

instances, implementation of solutions can be delayed by several months. The dialogue initiated between the program team and the complainant, and the mutual understanding between them have been of immense help to reduce the number of complaints and grievances that may escalate into higher levels of the GRM.

This team approach to problem solving has been recognized as one of the significant factors that contributed to the successful resolution of the project-related complaints and grievances. In Kegalle, it was reported that 97% of the complaints received have been resolved at the site level. In such instances, there was hardly any necessity to convene the higher-level GRCs for grievance

resolution. Of the complaints received by iRoad in Kegalle, only four were resolved at the GND-level GRC while its DSD-level GRC dealt with two complaints.

As mentioned, if an amicable settlement is not reached at the site level, the complaint is forwarded to the GND-level GRC. If issues cannot be settled at the GND level, they are directed to the DSD-level GRC. At the DSD level, if necessary, GRC members undertake joint site visits with the complainants to inspect the reported issues. Such visits are arranged by the DS (Figure 1).

In the event that the DSD-level GRC is still unable to resolve the issues, DS invites and consults other relevant authorities such as

Figure 1: Grievance Redress Process

Letter of Public Complaint

↓

Public Complaint Register
(Contractor)

↓

GRC Meeting
(Community, GN, PUI, PIC, Contractor)

↓

Minutes of the GRC Meeting

↓

Field visit with taking a decision to solve the problems
(Community, GN, PUI, PIC, Contractor)

GN = Grama Niladhari, GRC = Grievance Redress Committee, PIC = project implementation consultant, PIU = project implementation unit.

Source: Road Development Authority.

the chief secretary of the province or the chairperson of the Pradeshiya Sabha, or both.[17] The chief secretary or the chairperson of the Pradeshiya Sabha then talks with the complainants and tries to reach a settlement. There have been five such cases in the South that required intervention of the chief secretary or the Provincial Council. Some complex issues are also discussed at the meetings of the Provincial Council with the concurrence of the DS in order to arrive at best solutions. The time frame for grievance resolution at each GRC is 3 weeks from the date of the receipt of the grievance or complaint. Figure 2 presents the grievance redress flowchart.

Figure 2: Grievance Redress Flow Chart

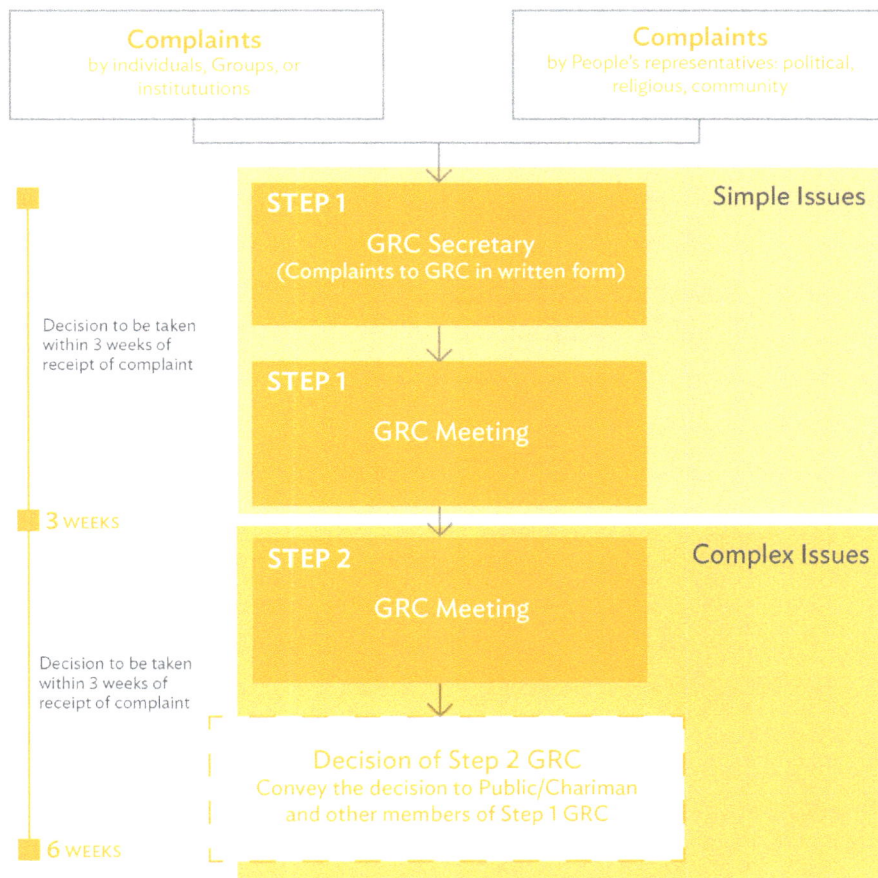

GRC = Grievance Redress Committee.

Source: Road Development Authority.

---

17 Pradeshiya Sabha is an elected local governance body at the lowest level providing a variety of local public services including roads, sanitation, drains, housing, libraries, public parks, and recreational facilities.

Types of Grievances, Complaints, Requests, and Suggestions Received

A review of the databases maintained in the Southern Province points to the need for better organization and clarity in segregating and documenting the issues falling into the four different categories. In some databases, e.g., in Galle District, issues are distinctly separated into four columns whereas in other databases, e.g., in Matara District, issues are listed under one single column, thus, making it difficult to recognize the exact category of the issues. Moreover, in some situations, issues have not been well documented leading to lack of clarity on the details and their respective category. A review of the summary of issues reported in the Matara District from July 2015 to April 2019 shows issues mainly resulting from construction-related impacts.

Table 3: Electronic Database of Complaints - Matara District

INTEGRATED ROAD INVESTMENT PROGRAM (iRoad)
PIC 1-SOUTHERN PROVINCE

Status of Public Complaints, Requests, Suggestions and Grievances
May 2015 to Dec 2018

District : Matara
Contract Package : M2

Complaint Ref. No.	Road ID	Road Name	Date of Complaint	Complaint received by (ie: Name and/or Designation of person/ Complaint Box, GRC etc.)	Complaint made in written/ verbal	Details of Complainer (Name, Address, Contact No/s.) etc.	Nature of Complaint (Brief description of complaint and chainage)	Status of Action Taken			Remarks (Satisfaction of complainer with the solution and/or other remarkable notes)
								Solution Agreed	Solution in Progress	Action Completed	
KDESH/IR/M2/RID-4/ESS/PC/001	4	Akurassa-Katanvila	23.06.2015	Project Manager, /KDESH	Written	Nihal Gunasekara,Nerahuwa	Request to raise inundating areas	Agreed to rise inundating area as appropriate level.	improved the road as requested. RDA & Consultant instructed for raising sections	Completed to the satisfaction of complainer	
KDESH/IR/M2/RID-4/ESS/PC/002	4	Akurassa-Katanvila	27.06.2015	EO/KDESH	Written	D. Vithanage, Iluppella, Akuressa.	Request for drains	Agreed to provide earth drain	improved the drain as requested. Consultant instructed to improve existing earth drain	Completed to the satisfaction of complainer	
KDESH/IR/M2/RID-4/ESS/PC/003	4	Akurassa-Katanvila	10.07.2015	EO, EO/KDESH	verbal	Secretary, Rural Development Society, Nerahuwa, Akuressa.	Inundating areas	inundating area to be improved to reduce flooding	improved inundating areas as requested.	Completed to the satisfaction of complainer	Verbal complain
KDESH/IR/M2/RID-4/ESS/PC/004	4	Akurassa-Katanvila	01.08.2015	Project Manager, EO/KDESH	Written	H.B. Wickramapala, Ruhunu Concrete Work, Imbulgoda, Akuressa.	To shift the Center Line	agreed to send the complaint to the client	unable to shift centerline as per the complainer request	Completed to the satisfaction of complainer	Complainer was made aware
KDESH/IR/M2/RID-1/ESS/PC/005	1	Kobugoda Road	30.07.2015	EO, EO/KDESH	verbal	M.V. Galis , Ihala Maliduwa, Ihalawtta, Akuressa.	Culvert Repairing 1+165	Agreed to repair culvert	improved culvert as requested.	Completed to the satisfaction of complainer	

July2015-April2019 CRACK ID-01 ID-02 ID-03 ID-04 ID-05 ID-06 ID-07 ID-40 ID-41 ID-42 ID-49 ID-50 ID-50A ID-51 ID-52 ID-53 ID-55 ID-56 ID-57

Source: Road Development Authority.

INTEGRATED ROAD INVESTMENT PROGRAM (iRoad)
PIC-01, SOUTHERN PROVINCE
Status of public Suggestions/Requests/Complaints/Grievances

District :Galle
Contract Package G2
Road Name : Hapugala Eriyagaha Junction
Road ID : 22

S/N	Requests	Suggestions	Complaints	Grievances
1	Requested a line drain infront of the school	Suggested to remove drain at 1+530 RHS	Complaint regarding eroded approach at 1+100 to 1+200 RHS	Dust agitation due to poor watering of ABC laid edge widening sections
2	Requested to continue the project to end of Eriyagaha Junction		Complaint for making access road muddy with machinery	Access has been damaged by a roler at 0+320 RHS
3	Requested to remove the brick wall at 0+545 to 0+565 RHS		Complained about the boundary wall collapsed & waer meter guage damaged due to excavation	Boundary wall and house cracked due to roller compaction at 0+340
4	Requested to remove the lottery counter at the beginning of the road		Complained about land inundate after road improvement	A gate has fallen at 0+160 RHS due to rain after excavation for drain
5	Requested to provide necessary drains suitable locations		Complained about dust agitation at 1+880	
6	Request to continue the u drain provided infront of land sale up to the culvert		Complained about exsisting drain removing at 0+200	
7	Requested to improve all culverts along the road, arrange proper access road		Complaint regarding raising culvert at 1+885	
8	Request for a new drain to prevent water flow		Complained about water stagnation	
9	Request to construct drains & improve the exixting access		Complained about about discharging water	

Source: Road Development Authority.

Issues submitted as segregated into the different categories are as follows:

Grievances

- Inconveniences due to the dust generated by construction,
- damages to graves,
- reduced safety of households, and
- flooding due to lack of or dysfunctional culverts and drainage system.

Complaints

- Cracks and damages caused to houses, business premises, public institutions, and their auxiliary structures due to vibration and use of heavy machinery;
- loss of access to houses, business premises, and public institutions such as schools and post offices due to raising the level of the roads;
- damages to water supply lines laid under road shoulders and those that provide water to residential units, and business premises;
- pollution of water in the wells located in lowlands from run-off mud water;
- storm water run-off entering houses and business premises;
- damages to paddy fields and drainage system around paddy fields;
- inundation of land; and
- objections to donate private land.

Requests

- Raise the level of the roads in areas that get inundated during rains,
- provide a proper drainage system,
- rehabilitate and widen the culverts to avoid flooding,
- shift the center line to avoid land donations,
- provide access to paddy fields, and
- raise and improve the house accesses.

Suggestions

- Remove the unsafe bends;
- construct retaining walls in areas vulnerable to earth slips or erosion,
- avoid cutting trees,
- clean the irrigation canals,
- cover the drains with concrete slabs,
- provide asphalted access to the temple adjacent to the road, and
- delay the construction work due to a pending court case.

Grievance Handling in the Southern Province and Kegalle District

Southern Province

The number of road projects implemented in the Southern Province was 183 with a total length of 591.3 kilometers (km). The program established 45 GRCs at the DSD level and 228 GRCs at the GND level. The semi annual social safeguards monitoring reports from July 2015 to June 2019 provide an overview of the number of grievances, complaints, requests, and suggestions received by the iRoad program and the status of their resolution. The Tables 5, 6, and 7 below provide the details.

Table 5: Grievances, Complaints, Requests, and Suggestions Reported by Affected People, 2015-2019

Galle District

Item	2015[18]	2016	2017	2018	2019[19]	Total
Grievances	39	11	12	0	0	62
Complaints	61	95	97	7	0	260
Requests	112	685	486	18	0	1,301
Suggestions	24	14	16	0	0	54
TOTAL	**236**	**805**	**611**	**25**	0	**1,677**

Matara District

Item	2015[20]	2016	2017	2018	2019[21]	Total
Grievances	0	3	11	0	0	14
Complaints	84	168	53	11	4	320
Requests	27	214	149	17	1	408
Suggestions	20	31	4	0	0	55
TOTAL	**131**	**416**	**217**	**28**	**5**	**797**

Hambantota District

Item	2015[22]	2016	2017	2018	2019[23]	Total
Grievances	1	13	0	0	0	14
Complaints	29	61	35	3	1	129
Requests	36	422	259	7	0	724
Suggestions	10	6	5	0	0	21
TOTAL	**76**	**502**	**299**	**10**	**1**	**888**

Southern Province

Item	2015[24]	2016	2017	2018	2019[25]	Total
Grievances	40	27	23	0	0	90
Complaints	174	324	185	21	5	709
Requests	175	1,321	894	42	1	2,433
Suggestions	54	51	25	0	0	130
TOTAL	**443**	**1,723**	**1,127**	**63**	**6**	**3,362**

Source: Road Development Authority.

[18] July–December 2015.
[19] January–June 2019.
[20] July–December 2015.
[21] January–June 2019.
[22] July–December 2015.
[23] January–June 2019.
[24] July–December 2015.
[25] January–June 2019.

Table 6: Status of Grievance Resolution

Galle District

Item	2015[26]	2016	2017	2018	2019[27]	Total
Grievances, complaints, requests, and suggestions received	236	805	611	25	0	1,677
Solutions in progress[28]	172	388	168	2	0	730
Grievances, complaints, requests, and suggestions resolved	64	417	443	23	0	947
Grievances, complaints, requests, and suggestions resolved at project site level	54	345	363	16	0	778
Grievances, complaints, requests, and suggestions resolved at GND level	9	67	72	7	0	155
Grievances, complaints, requests, and suggestions resolved at DSD level	1	5	7	0	0	13
Grievances, complaints, requests, and suggestions resolved at PC level	**0**	**0**	**1**	**0**	**0**	**1**

Matara District

Item	2015[29]	2016	2017	2018	2019[30]	Total
Grievances, complaints, requests, and suggestions received	131	416	217	28	5	797
Solutions in progress[31]	69	186	91	2	0	348
Grievances, complaints, requests, and suggestions resolved	62	230	126	26	5	449
Grievances, complaints, requests, and suggestions resolved at project site level	53	165	75	18	2	313
Grievances, complaints, requests, and suggestions resolved at GND level	7	42	41	8	0	98
Grievances, complaints, requests, and suggestions resolved at DSD level	2	23	8	0	2	35
Grievances, complaints, requests, and suggestions resolved at PC level	**0**	**0**	**2**	**0**	**1**	**3**

continued on next page

[26] July–December 2015.
[27] January–June 2019.
[28] The number of unresolved complaints, grievances, requests, and suggestions at the end of each reporting period. However, at the project conclusion in June 2019, all outstanding complaints, grievances, requests, and suggestions have been addressed, and the numbers have been reduced to zero.
[29] July–December 2015.
[30] January–June 2019.
[31] Indicate the number of unresolved complaints, grievances, requests, and suggestions at the end of each reporting period. However, at the project conclusion in June 2019, all outstanding complaints, grievances, requests and suggestions had been addressed, and the numbers have been reduced to zero.

Table 6: Status of Grievance Resolution

Hambantota District

Item	2015[32]	2016	2017	2018	2019[33]	Total
Grievances, complaints, requests, and suggestions received	76	502	299	10	1	888
Solutions in progress[34]	17	269	54	1	0	341
Grievances, complaints, requests, and suggestions resolved	59	233	245	9	1	547
Grievances, complaints, requests, and suggestions resolved at project site level	46	177	172	6	1	402
Grievances, complaints, requests, and suggestions resolved at GND level	13	45	60	3	0	121
Grievances, complaints, requests, and suggestions resolved at DSD level	0	11	12	0	0	23
Grievances, complaints, requests, and suggestions resolved at PC level	0	0	1	0	0	1

DSD = Divisional Secretary's Division, GND = Grama Niladhari Division, PC= Provincial Council.

Source: Road Development Authority

Table 7: Status of Grievance Redress Committee Meetings Conducted

Type	2015[35]	2016	2017	2018	2019[36]	Total
Galle District						
GND Level	None	None	106	14	0	120
DSD Level	None	None	34	0	0	34
PC Level	None	None	1	0	0	1
TOTAL			141	14	0	155
Matara District						
GND Level	None	None	109	20	0	129
DSD Level	None	None	37	0	2	39
PC Level	None	None	2	0	0	2
TOTAL			148	20	2	170
Hambantota District						
GND Level	None	None	91	7	0	98
DSD Level	None	None	12	0	0	12
PC Level	None	None	1	0	0	1
TOTAL			104	7	0	111
Southern Province						
GND Level	None	None	306	41	0	347
DSD Level	None	None	83	0	2	85
PC Level	None	None	4	0	0	4
TOTAL			393	41	2	436

DSD = Divisional Secretary's Division, GND = Grama Niladhari Division, PC= Provincial Council.

Source: Road Development Authority

[32] July–December 2015.
[33] January–June 2019.
[34] Indicate the number of unresolved complaints, grievances, requests, and suggestions at the end of each reporting period. However, at the project conclusion in June 2019, all outstanding grievances, complaints, requests, and suggestions had been addressed, and the numbers have been reduced to zero.
[35] July–December 2015.
[36] January–June 2019.

Kegalle District

The total number of road projects implemented in the Kegalle District is 63 with a total length of 217 km. The program has set up 11 DSD-level GRCs and 108 GND-level GRCs. The cumulative number of complaints, crack-related issues, requests, and suggestions reported in the Kegalle District from December 2015 to July 2019 is shown in Table 8.

Of the issues reported, 720 complaints, requests, and suggestions have been resolved completely. The remaining 174 are to be resolved at the time of this study. Some case examples are included in the Appendix.

Monitoring and Reporting

The project engineer presents a summary report of the complaints received and the status of their resolution during the monthly progress review meetings of the project.

The TA consultant and the Environmental and Social Development Division (ESDD) undertake periodic monitoring of both the process and the outcomes of the grievance management. They conduct these monitoring exercises either individually or jointly. The safeguards specialists of PIC also carry out on-site social safeguards monitoring to ensure that grievances and complaints are addressed in a timely manner. Likewise, the Sri Lanka Resident Mission conducts periodic monitoring. Monitoring results are included in the bi-annual social monitoring reports. The preliminary status reports, initially prepared by the environment officer and the project engineer, are submitted to the resident engineer for review. The resident engineer then submits these to the team leader of the PIC. The PIC staff prepares the final report and shares it with the project directors of the PIUs, resident mission, TA consultant, ESDD, project management unit of the RDA, and the chief secretary of the province.

Table 8: Cumulative Number of Complaints in Kegalle District

Complaints	Requests	Suggestions	Total
469	380	45	894

Source: Road Development Authority.

III. Lessons Learned

Community participation in resolving a complaint in iRoad
Sabaragamuwa province (photo by RDA).

Studies and evaluations conducted on STDP highlighted several gaps such as: (i) inadequate consultation and information sharing with potential APs on changes to the project design during implementation and its potential impacts on them, (ii) failure to revise and update the environmental and social impact assessments based on the design change, (iii) insufficient identification and definition of poor and vulnerable persons and households, and (iv) lack of viable and effective communication strategy from early stages of project preparation. As a result, rumors spread rapidly, and APs received wrong/misleading information about the project and its impact driving them to protest and/or to resort to legal action. In this context, the institutions intervened to address the issues such as the Supreme Court, the Court of Appeal, and ADB's OSPF and CRP stated that *'the RDA had not adequately consulted the APs to understand their views on the expressway and its designs, and to share project information, details of APs' entitlements, and how the project would affect them....The Supreme Court awarded compensation for the violation of the APs' fundamental right to know and right to be informed, as guaranteed by the country's Constitution' (p. 225).*[37] Moreover, the project completion report of STDP also observed that: *'Managing the public relationship is an important part of successful project management. Even with the best ever compensation package in Sri Lanka, strong public protests were faced at the beginning of the project with regard to land acquisition and compensation process. A proper project communication plan was not prepared during the project formulation and early implementation stage' (p. 14).*[38] Learning from that experience, iRoad took a different position with its bottom-up approach and a major drive on information sharing and community consultations on different aspects of road improvements. In this regard, the program has enormously invested in raising awareness and sensitizing the staff of the project implementing agency, project consultants, and the contractor (a majority of whom are engineering and technical cadres) on the strategic importance of community engagement, consultations, and information sharing in all phases of the project implementation. This transformative approach is embedded in one of the concepts adopted by iRoad and is introduced as context-sensitive design (CSD) which provides for a mandatory requirement on the part of project designers, planners, and implementers to commence their respective tasks with community consultations and information sharing. The program adopts a number of methodologies to consult the communities. They include transect walks in the project areas, focus group discussions with community members, individual interviews, and grievance redress meetings. These consultations allow the community members to express their issues and concerns over road improvement projects, present their additional requests and suggestions, as well as share their local knowledge particularly on environmental aspects with the project designers, planners, and implementers. iRoad also ensures that valuable suggestions and requests forwarded by the communities are incorporated into the road improvement designs wherever possible.

---

[37] ADB. 2016. *Challenges in Implementing Best Practices in Involuntary Resettlement A Case Study in Sri Lanka.* Manila.
[38] ADB. 2014. *Completion Report: Southern Transport Development Project in Sri Lanka.* Manila.

This section derives some key features and lessons learned from the grievance redress and problem-solving experiences of iRoad. They are as follows:

(i) iRoad has a project-based GRM, the legitimacy of which was derived from the project's resettlement framework approved by the Government of Sri Lanka. The GRM strengthened its legitimacy by engaging two local level government officers, the GN and the DS, chairing its two-tier GRCs.

(ii) The engagement of the GN to lead the GND-level GRC, and the DS as the chairperson of the DSD-level GRC has brought added recognition and legitimacy to the grievance redress and problem-solving process in the iRoad program. On the other hand, the engagement resulted in personal recognition and esteem to these public officers who serve the GRM and contributed to building a sense of ownership in project implementation and management. Moreover, the involvement of other village- and divisional-level public officers by the GN and the DS in consultations and problem-solving processes has, directly and indirectly, contributed to their extended support for the effective implementation of the iRoad program.

(iii) The GRM brings together various stakeholders such as government administrators, service providing agencies, local-level development officers, civil society organizations, religious leaders, and a strong female representation to engage in a collective effort to resolve their issues and problems in coordination with project implementers. As such, it provides an effective forum for citizens' engagement which can also provide valuable inputs to the project design and planning, participation in project implementation, and monitoring. As the case study shows, some grievances cannot be resolved in isolation by a single party but requires the participation and intervention of various stakeholders, and their commitment for resource allocations.

(iv) Each level of the GRM has authority to decide on the complaints and grievances, which shortens turnaround time for solving complaints and grievances.

(v) The GRM is efficient and effective, significantly contributing to the timeliness in addressing the grievances and complaints of the affected people at the project site and preventing their escalation to higher levels. It also provides a cost-effective, accessible, and credible process, specifically for poor communities and households to resolve their grievances locally without moving into costly legal procedures.

(vi) The project staff and consultants of iRoad listen and consider the requests and suggestions received from the villagers who appreciate this gesture. This helps minimize the complaints or grievances that revert to the project at a later stage.

(vii) The endeavors of the iRoad staff and safeguards teams, contractors, and consultants to resolve the grievances at the site level, working as a team and responding efficiently to the issues raised, are remarkable as these not only provide quick solutions to the problems but also strengthen the mutual understanding, trust, and confidence between the AP and the project implementers. As the GN of Pananwela West observed, "GRCs are good, because they strengthen the relationship between the villagers and the contractor. Also, when various requests are made by the GN or the DS on behalf of the communities, the contractors respond to them positively. Villagers asked for culverts in places that get inundated. Engineers did not have this local knowledge as they are outsiders. But they listened to the villagers, appreciated the local knowledge, and constructed the culverts. This mechanism helped resolve problems quickly. This is a good model for replication in other similar projects. The openness and cooperative spirit between the communities and contractors enabled the easy flow of communication and information, contributing to the timely resolution of grievances and to the satisfaction of affected people."

(viii) iRoad did not involve any involuntary land acquisitions. Neither did it have any provision to pay cash compensation except for material assistance for the rehabilitation and restoration of damaged properties, most of which were shouldered by the contractor. As such, grievances and complaints in the iRoad program were largely the non-cash compensation-based issues for which a project-based efficient GRM can appropriately resolve.

(ix) The processes followed by iRoad to disseminate information and get the community engaged are a noteworthy feature of the program to raise community awareness on the existence and the functioning of the GRM. Lack of community awareness on GRM can cause people seeking redress from undue sources and potential disruptions to project-implementing processes. Done as early as the project design stage, the programs created an atmosphere of trust between the affected parties, project-implementing agencies, contractors, and other stakeholders. This trust contributed to the efficient and effective implementation of the project GRM and timely resolution of grievances and complaints.

(x) The CSD approach, a unique feature of iRoad, has immensely contributed to community consultation, engagement, and participation throughout the project cycle, and to building a sense of community ownership to the project. The approach has also been serving as an effective mechanism to prevent or, at least minimize, complaints and grievances, thereby facilitating the smooth implementation of the project.

(xi) iRoad provided adequate resources to the GRM. Apart from the large cadre of environmental and social safeguards teams assigned by the program to manage safeguards and address grievances, the program also invested substantial amounts of financial resources to respond to the additional needs of the communities. In the Southern Province, the project invested more than SLR389.70 million to accommodate the requests and suggestions to change the road designs. In the Kegalle District, the total amount spent on meeting public requests was more than SLR16.20 million. Addressing these requests the best possible way enabled the iRoad program to minimize the complaints and grievances.

(xii) GRM-related databases, particularly when large projects like iRoad are handled, need to be improved with management information systems, proper recording of the details of the complaint, and efficient retrieval systems.

Neither a project-based GRM nor a legally instituted GRM can resolve the grievances resulting from the iRoad project. Both require additional support outside their mandate to address the grievances. In iRoad, this complementary role was efficiently performed by the field-level project staff who significantly contributed to reduce the number of grievances and complaints that would have been otherwise reported to the formal GRM.

Grievance resolution is not a one-off activity. As the case pointed out, it requires several rounds of discussion and negotiations, compromise between concerned parties, and reaching agreements to share resources and contribute to the problem-solving process.

Appendix

Appendix: iRoad Cases

This appendix presents a few examples of grievance resolution outcomes as reported by project staff as well as those derived from interviews conducted with the complainants and during field visits.

Case No. 1: On Hathagala Road in Hambantota, there was a 300-meter (m) section where the road passes beside a tank bund. Rehabilitation work required elevating and asphalting the road. On one side of the road were paddy fields while on the other side were paddy fields and settlements. There were two opposing parties—one party favored raising the road while the other opposed to it as doing so may make their lands susceptible to flood. There was an irrigation canal beside the road which was not enough to drain storm water as water flow was blocked by accumulated solid waste. The Irrigation Department (ID) requested the Road Development Authority (RDA) to use its funds to improve the canal. However, RDA neither had the mandate nor the funds to restore the entire canal. A meeting was held between the Divisional Secretary (DS) and the complainants but did not yield results. The second meeting also ended without reaching a solution. The ID could not do much to help in grievance resolution. After four rounds of meetings, an agreement was reached between RDA and ID. RDA agreed to widen the canal width only at the location where the canal underpasses the road and to rehabilitate the existing culvert. ID agreed to restore the sluice gate of the canal and remove the blockages. DS recorded this decision which was communicated to the complainants. With the canal widening and improvements, water flow improved, and RDA was able to raise the level of the road.

Case No. 2: On Handunkatuwa–Eraminiya Road in Hambantota, there was a 500 m section which required concreting. Villagers opposed the concreting and instead they asked for an asphalt pavement. The engineers tried to explain to them why the road could not be asphalted, citing as reasons the weak soil condition and the frequent flooding. Though some people agreed to the explanations, others did not. In previous projects, these villagers experienced poor-quality work by contractors in road concreting, and they feared that the same would happen here as well. The case was reported to the DS, and the assistant director for planning representing the DS likewise iterated to the villagers the reasons for not asphalting the road section. Still, some did not agree, and they approached the local politician. The program conducted several rounds of awareness-raising programs to convince the villagers, at the end of which, except for one person, the rest of the villagers consented to concreting. The DS personally spoke to the person who continued to oppose, and finally the road concreting was completed.

Case No. 3: There was a culvert on Godawaya Road in Hambantota which was not functioning properly because a household had put stones inside and over the culvert to prevent run-off storm water from entering his garden. This led to a conflict between the person who blocked the culvert and the others in the neighborhood as run-off storm water instead entered into their gardens particularly during heavy rains. The case was reported to the Grama Niladhari (GN) who invited the chairman of the Paradeshiya Sabha to confirm the report. The household who blocked the culvert asked for a concrete drain to divert the water flow to a nearby marshy land. The opposing party also requested that storm water be diverted via a newly constructed concrete drain. The program did not have the financial provisions to construct a drain and proposed to install only a hume pipe. As the conflict between the two parties continued and the GN was unable to resolve the issue, the DS was invited to intervene. The DS contacted the disaster management unit of his division, but they could not propose a suitable solution as well. As a result, construction work in this section was delayed by 7 months. The DS negotiated with the program to construct the drain along the culvert section in the meantime that he was securing the funds (SLR1.2 million) to complete rest of the drain. More than 15 meetings were held to resolve the issue.

Case No. 4: The standard surface width prescribed for iRoad projects is 3 m. The Wilpita–Uggahahena Road in Matara with a length of 3.5 kilometers (km) was only 2 m wide, necessitating road widening. In one section of this road, one household had built a retaining wall that constrained widening. This household was not willing to demolish his retaining wall or to donate extra land for road widening. Thus, the program decided to take a portion of the land owned by the household living at the opposite side of this retaining wall. However, he argued that additional land required for road widening should be taken from both sides, and not just from a single side.

This complainant said:

> "this retaining wall owner had encroached 2 feet from road reservation to construct the wall. RDA is trying to take land from our side. We have no objection to the road. The DS now decided to rehabilitate the road within the existing width without any widening. If this happened, we will not get a good road. If court decide to demolish the wall, we will have fewer problems. We have complained to the DS, Pradeshiya Sabha, and project engineer. They all requested that we donate our land as the road is important to the villagers. But we told them that it is unfair to take only our land without any land donation from the retaining wall owner. In the end, Pradeshiya Sabha filed a court case against the household that built the retaining wall on encroached land."

The other villagers verified that this retaining wall had, indeed, been built on encroached road reservation. The program had no authority to demolish the wall or to pay compensation to re-construct the retaining wall in the remaining portion of the land. The Grama Niladhari Division (GND)-level Grievance Redress Committee (GRC) could not resolve the issue. The case was reported to the Divisional Secretary's Division (DSD)-level GRC, and the DS invited the chairman of the Pradeshiya Sabha to participate in the resolution process. The household who owned the retaining wall did not participate in the resolution process. However, he objected to removing the wall and thus, a settlement could not be reached. In the end, the Pradeshiya Sabha decided to file a court case requesting the demolition of this illegally constructed retaining wall. The decision of the court is still pending at the time of this study. Meanwhile, the project will continue with road rehabilitation work confining its civil works to the existing right of way. If the court grants permission to remove the wall, Pradeshiya Sabha will use its own funds.

Case No. 5: Aranayaka–Sapumalambe–Welanthalawa Road in the Kegalle District with a length of 2.1 km was a narrow road and required widening. Land donations were required from the residents. One household, though he liked donating the land from his property, expressed refusal to demolish his retaining wall without receiving adequate compensation from the program to construct a wall in the remaining portion of the land. The program did not have the resources to construct the retaining wall or to pay cash compensation. Instead, but only after much persuasion, the household living at the opposite side of this retaining wall agreed to donate the land from his own property.

Case No. 6: A household living below the D C Abeywickrema Road in Matara was affected by the road rehabilitation work. The road did not have side drains, and the soil removed for rehabilitation work was piled beside the road. When it rained, run-off storm water and mud entered the property of this household leading to the collapse of her retaining wall, mud inside her house, and damage to her orchids. The loss was estimated at SLR45,000. The complaint was resolved at the DSD-level GRC with the project agreeing to construct a new retaining wall for the household as well as a drain by the side of the road to ensure that the property would be secured and that she would not be affected by run-off storm water in the future. The complainant was satisfied with the resolution.

Case No. 7: The rehabilitation work of 1.2 km Beragala–Paragammana–Dikella Road in the Kegalle District caused damages to a drinking water well that was located beside the road. The well was situated below the road. The damage was caused when the backhoe machine used for civil works struck the concrete structure of the well resulting in run-off mud water from the road to enter the well polluting its water. Thus, the household could not use the water. The complainant reported the incident to the project director. In response to her complaint, the assistant resident engineer together with the project engineer, construction engineer, and the environment officer of the contractor met the complainant and assured complete restoration of the damaged well. The complaint was resolved at site level. In addition to full restoration of the well, the project also provided concrete slabs to cover the surface of the well. The complainant was happy with the restoration work and remarked that "it is now better than what it was; and I offer merit (*pin sidda venava*) for all those who helped me."

Case No. 8: The construction of a drain along the Aranayaka–Sapumalambe–Welanthalawa Road in the Kegalle District caused damages to a retaining wall of a household. Cracks also began to appear on his land, creating an unsafe environment for the household. The grievance was reported to the project director and, in consideration of the insecure status of the household, the project provided a retaining wall.

Case No. 9: One section of the Aranayaka–Sapumalambe–Welanthalawa Road in the Kegalle District passes through the temple premises of the Aranayaka Udagama Bodhimalu Viharaya. This caused disturbances to the temple activities as well as to its devotees. During the road construction work, both the priest and the villagers requested a change in the design of the road to avoid it traversing the temple property. Adequate temple land was available for road diversion. The project agreed to alter the design, and with permission from the ministry, the road was diverted to traverse behind the temple instead. Both the priest and the villagers were satisfied with the project's compliance to their request. The GN of the area recalled, "the road was the prime need of the people. They never raised objections or grievances. In fact, they very much supported the construction work, and sometimes provided meals to the construction workers."

Case No. 10: The construction work of the D C Abeywickrema Road in Matara involved raising the road level. This had caused run-off storm water to enter the gardens of the households living beside the road. The issue was reported to the contractor who agreed to construct a drain covered with concrete slabs. However, at the time of the case study, the problem has not been resolved completely, and run-off storm water still enters the properties of the households. Moreover, the main water line and its service connections to households were concealed under the concrete drain depriving the households to carry out any repair work during breakdowns or leakages. Though the affected households had reported the situation to both the contractor and the National Water Supply and Drainage Board, the response they received was that they did not have any alternative.

www.ingramcontent.com/pod-product-compliance
Lightning Source LLC
Chambersburg PA
CBHW050057220326
41599CB00045B/7445